Concerning the Nature of Good, Against the Manichaeans

Concerning the Nature of Good, Against the Manichaeans

St. Augustine

Concerning the Nature of Good, Against the Manichaeans

© Lighthouse Publishing 2018

Written by: St. Augustine (Nov.13 354 – Aug.28 430)

Translated by: Albert H. Newman, D.D., L.L.D.

Updated into Modern U.S English by A.M. Overett (b. 1960)

All rights reserved. Without limiting the rights under copyright reserved above, no part of this publication may be reproduced, stored in a retrieval system, or transmitted, in any form or by any means (electronic, mechanical, photocopying, recording or otherwise), without the prior written permission of the copyright owner of this book.

Published by
Lighthouse Christian Publishing
SAN 257-4330
5531 Dufferin Drive
Savage, Minnesota, 55378
United States of America

www.lighthousechristianpublishing.com

Written after the year 404. It is put in the Retractations immediately after the De Actis cum Felice Manichæo, which was written about the end of the year 404. It is one of the most argumentative of the Anti-Manichæan treatises, and so one of the most abstruse and difficult. The lines of argument here pursued have already been employed in part in the earlier treatises. The most interesting portions of the contents of the treatise, and the most damaging to the Manichæans, are the long extracts from Mani's Thesaurus, and his Fundamental Epistle. —A.H.N.

Chapter 1. —God the Highest and Unchangeable Good, from Whom are All Other Good Things, Spiritual and Corporeal.

The highest good, than which there is no higher, is God, and consequently He is unchangeable good, hence truly eternal and truly immortal. All other good things are only from Him, not of Him. For what is of Him, is Himself. And consequently if He alone is unchangeable, all things that He has made, because He has made them out of nothing, are changeable. For He is so omnipotent, that even out of nothing, that is out of what is absolutely non-existent, He can make good things both great and small, both celestial and terrestrial, both spiritual and corporeal. But because He is also just, He has not put those things that He has made out of nothing on an equality with that which He begat out of Himself. Because, therefore, no good things whether great or small, through whatever gradations of things, can exist except from God; but since every nature, so far as it is nature, is good, it follows that no nature can exist save from the most high and true God: because all things even not in the highest degree good, but related to the highest good, and again, because all good things, even those of most recent origin, which are far from the highest good, can have their existence only from the highest good. Therefore, every spirit, though subject to change, and every corporeal entity, is from God, and all this, having been made, is nature. For every nature is either spirit or body. Unchangeable spirit is God, changeable spirit, having been made, is nature, but is better than body; but body is not spirit, unless when the wind, because it is invisible to us and yet its power is felt as something not inconsiderable, is in a certain sense called spirit.

Chapter 2. —How This May Suffice for Correcting the Manichæans.

But for the sake of those who, not being able to understand that all nature, that is, every spirit and everybody, is naturally good, are moved by the iniquity of spirit and the mortality of body, and on this account endeavor to bring in another nature of wicked spirit and mortal body, which God did not make, we determine thus to bring to their understanding what we say can be brought. For they acknowledge that no good thing can exist save from the highest and true God, which also is true and suffices for correcting them, if they are willing to give heed.

Chapter 3. —Measure, Form, and Order, Generic Goods in Things Made by God.

For we Catholic Christians worship God, from whom are all good things whether great or small; from whom is all measure great or small; from whom is all form great or small; from whom is all order great or small. For all things in proportion as they are better measured, formed, and ordered, are assuredly good in a higher degree; but in proportion as they are measured, formed, and ordered in an inferior degree, are they the less good. These three things, therefore, measure, form, and order, —not to speak of innumerable other things that are shown to pertain to these three, —these three things, therefore, measure, form, order, are as it were generic goods in things made by God, whether in spirit or in body. God is, therefore, above every measure of the creature, above every form, above every order, nor is He above by local spaces, but by ineffable and singular potency, from whom is every measure, every form, every order. These three things, where they are great, are great goods, where they are small, are small goods; where they are absent, there is no good. And again, where these things are great, there are great natures, where they are small, there are small natures, where they are absent, there is no nature. Therefore all nature is good.

Chapter 4. —Evil is Corruption of Measure, Form, or Order.

When accordingly it is inquired, whence is evil, it must first be inquired, what is evil, which is nothing else than corruption, either of the measure, or the form, or the order, that belong to nature. Nature therefore which has been corrupted, is called evil, for assuredly when incorrupt it is good; but even when corrupt, so far as it is nature it is good, so far as it is corrupted it is evil.

Chapter 5. —The Corrupted Nature of a More Excellent Order Sometimes Better Than an Inferior Nature Even Uncorrupted.

But it may happen, that a certain nature which has been ranked as more excellent by reason of natural measure and form, though corrupt, is even yet better than another incorrupt which has been ranked lower by reason of an inferior natural measure and form: as in the estimation of men, according to the quality which presents itself to view, corrupt gold is assuredly better than incorrupt silver, and corrupt silver than incorrupt lead; so also in more powerful spiritual natures a rational spirit even corrupted through an evil will is better than an irrational though incorrupt, and better is any spirit whatever even corrupt than anybody whatever though incorrupt. For better is a nature which, when it is present in a body, furnishes it with life, than that to which life is furnished. But however corrupt may be the spirit of life that has been made, it can furnish life to a body, and hence, though corrupt, it is better than the body though incorrupt.

Chapter 6. —Nature Which Cannot Be Corrupted is the Highest Good; That Which Can, is Some Good.

But if corruption take away all measure, all form, all order from corruptible things, no nature will remain. And consequently, every nature which cannot be corrupted is the highest good, as is God. But every nature that can be corrupted is also itself some good; for corruption cannot injure it, except by taking away from or diminishing that which is good.

Chapter 7. —The Corruption of Rational Spirits is on the One Hand Voluntary, on the Other Penal.

But to the most excellent creatures, that is, to rational spirits, God has offered this, that if they will not they cannot be corrupted; that is, if they should maintain obedience under the Lord their God, so should they adhere to his incorruptible beauty; but if they do not will to maintain obedience, since willingly they are corrupted in sins, unwillingly they shall be corrupted in punishment, since God is such a good that it is well for no one who deserts Him, and among the things made by God the rational nature is so great a good, that there is no good by which it may be blessed except God. Sinners, therefore, are ordained to punishment; which ordination is punishment because it is not conformable to their nature, but it is justice because it is conformable to their fault.

Chapter 8. —From the Corruption and Destruction of Inferior Things is the Beauty of the Universe.

But the rest of things that are made of nothing, which are assuredly inferior to the rational soul, can be neither blessed nor miserable. But because in proportion to their fashion and appearance are things themselves good, nor could there be good things in a less or the least degree except from God, they are so ordered that the more infirm yield to the firmer, the weaker to the stronger, the more impotent to the more powerful; and so earthly things harmonize with celestial, as being subject to the things that are pre-eminent. But to things falling away, and succeeding, a certain temporal beauty in its kind belongs, so that neither those things that die, or cease to be what they were, degrade or disturb the fashion and appearance and order of the universal creation; as a speech well composed is assuredly beautiful, although in it syllables and all sounds rush past as it were in being born and in dying.

Chapter 9. —Punishment is Constituted for the Sinning Nature that It May Be Rightly Ordered.

What sort of punishment, and how great, is due to

each fault, belongs to Divine judgment, not to human; which punishment assuredly when it is remitted in the case of the converted, there is great goodness on the part of God, and when it is deservedly inflicted, there is no injustice on the part of God; because nature is better ordered by justly smarting under punishment than by rejoicing with impunity in sin; which nature nevertheless, even thus having some measure, form, and order, in whatever extremity there is as yet some good, which things, if they were absolutely taken away, and utterly consumed, there will be accordingly no good, because no nature will remain.

Chapter 10. —Natures Corruptible, Because Made of Nothing.

All corruptible natures therefore are natures at all only so far as they are from God, nor would they be corruptible if they were of Him; because they would be what He himself is. Therefore of whatever measure, of whatever form, of whatever order, they are, they are so because it is God by whom they were made; but they are not immutable, because it is nothing of which they were made. For it is sacrilegious audacity to make nothing and God equal, as when we wish to make what has been born of God such as what has been made by Him out of nothing.

Chapter 11. —God Cannot Suffer Harm, Nor Can Any Other Nature Except by His Permission.

Wherefore neither can God's nature suffer harm, nor can any nature under God suffer harm unjustly: for when by sinning unjustly some do harm, an unjust will is imputed to them; but the power by which they are permitted to do harm is from God alone, who knows, while they themselves are ignorant, what they ought to suffer, whom He permits them to harm.

Chapter 12. —All Good Things are from God Alone. All these things are so perspicuous, so assured, that if they who introduce another nature which God did not make, were willing to give attention, they would not be filled with so great blasphemies, as that they should place so great good things in supreme evil, and so great evil things in God. For what the truth compels them to acknowledge, namely, that all good things are from God alone, suffices for their correction, if they were willing to give heed, as I said above. Not, therefore, are great good things from one, and small good things from another; but good things great and small are from the supremely good alone, which is God.

Chapter 13. —Individual Good Things, Whether Small or Great, are from God.

Let us, therefore, bring before our minds good things however great, which it is fitting that we attribute to God as their author, and these having been eliminated let us see whether any nature will remain. All life both great and small, all power great and small, all safety great and small, all memory great and small, all virtue great and small, all intellect great and small, all tranquility great and small, all plenty great and small, all sensation great and small, all light great and small, all suavity great and small, all measure great and small, all beauty great and small, all peace great and small, and whatever other like things may occur, especially such as are found throughout all things, whether spiritual or corporeal, every measure, every form, every order both great and small, are from the Lord God. All which good things whoever should wish to abuse, pays the penalty by divine judgment; but where none of these things shall have been present at all, no nature will remain.

Chapter 14. —Small Good Things in Comparison with Greater are Called by Contrary Names.

But in all these things, whatever are small are called by contrary names in comparison with greater things; as in the form of a man because the beauty is greater, the beauty of the ape in comparison with it is called deformity. And the imprudent are deceived, as if the former is good, and the latter evil, nor do they regard in the body of the ape its own fashion, the equality of members on both sides, the agreement of parts, the protection of safety, and other things which it would be tedious to enumerate.

Chapter 15. —In the Body of the Ape the Good of Beauty is Present, Though in a Less Degree.

But that what we have said may be understood, and may satisfy those too slow of comprehension, or that even the pertinacious and those repugnant to the most manifest truth may be compelled to confess what is true, let them be asked, whether corruption can harm the body of an ape? But if it can, so that it may become more hideous, what diminishes but the good of beauty?

Whence as long as the nature of the body subsists, so long something will remain. If, accordingly, good having been consumed, nature is consumed, the nature is therefore good. So also we say that slow is contrary to swift, but yet he who does not move at all cannot even be called slow. So we say that a heavy voice is contrary to a sharp voice, or a harsh to a musical; but if you completely remove any kind of voice, there is silence where there is no voice, which silence, nevertheless, for the simple reason that there is no voice, is usually opposed to voice as something contrary thereto. So also lucid and obscure are called as it were two contrary things, yet even obscure things have something of light, which being absolutely wanting, darkness is the absence of light in the same way in which silence is the absence of voice.

Chapter 16. —Privations in Things are Fittingly Ordered by God.

Yet even these privations of things are so ordered in the universe of nature, that to those wisely considering they not unfittingly have their vicissitudes. For by not illuminating certain places and times, God has also made the darkness as fittingly as the day. For if we by restraining the voice fittingly interpose silence in speaking, how much more does He, as the perfect framer of all things, fittingly make privations of things? Whence also in the hymn of the three children, light and darkness alike praise God, that is, bring forth praise in the hearts of those who well consider.

Chapter 17. —Nature, in as Far as It is Nature, No Evil.

No nature, therefore, as far as it is nature, is evil; but to each nature there is no evil except to be diminished in respect of good. But if by being diminished it should be consumed so that there is no good, no nature would be left; not only such as the Manichæans introduce, where so great good things are found that their exceeding blindness is wonderful, but such as anyone can introduce.

Chapter 18. —Hyle, Which Was Called by the Ancients the Formless Material of Things, is Not an Evil.

For neither is that material, which the ancients called Hyle, to be called an evil. I do not say that which Manichæus with most senseless vanity, not knowing what he says, denominates Hyle, namely, the former of corporeal beings; whence it is rightly said to him, that he introduces another god. For nobody can form and create corporeal beings but God alone; for neither are they created unless there subsist with them measure, form, and order, which I think that now even they themselves confess to be good things, and things that cannot be except from God. But by Hyle I mean a certain material absolutely formless and without quality, whence those qualities that we perceive are formed, as the ancients said. For hence also wood is called in Greek ὕλη, because it is adapted to workmen, not that itself may make anything, but that it is the material of which something may be made. Nor is that Hyle, therefore, to be called an evil which cannot be perceived through any appearance, but can scarcely be thought of through any sort of privation of appearance. For this has also a capacity of forms; for if it cannot receive the form imposed by the workman, neither assuredly may it be called material. Hence if form is some good, whence those who excel in it are called beautiful, as from appearance they are called handsome, even the capacity of form is undoubtedly something good. As because wisdom is a good, no one doubts that to be capable of wisdom is a good. And because every good is from God, no one ought to doubt that even matter, if there is any, has its existence from God alone.

Chapter 19. —To Have True Existence is an Exclusive Prerogative of God.

Magnificently and divinely, therefore, our God said to his servant: "I am that I am," and "Thou shalt say to the children of Israel, He who is sent me to you." For He truly is because He is unchangeable. For every change makes what was not, to be: therefore He truly is, who is unchangeable; but all other things that were made by Him have received being from Him each in its own measure. To Him who is highest, therefore nothing can be contrary, save what is not; and consequently, as from Him everything that is good has its being, so from Him is everything that by nature exists; since everything that exists by nature is good. Thus every nature is good, and everything good is from God; therefore every nature is from God.

Chapter 20. —Pain Only in Good Natures.

But pain which some supposed to be in an especial manner an evil, whether it be in mind or in body, cannot exist except in good natures. For the very fact of resistance in any being leading to pain, involves a refusal not to be what it was, because it was something good; but when a being is compelled to something better, the pain is useful, when to something worse, it is useless. Therefore in the case of the mind, the will resisting a greater power causes pain; in the case of the body, sensation resisting a more powerful body causes pain. But evils without pain are worse: for it is worse to rejoice iniquity than to bewail corruption; yet even such rejoicing cannot exist save from the attainment of inferior good things. But iniquity is the desertion of better things. Likewise in a body, a wound with pain is better than painless putrescence, which is especially called the corruption which the dead flesh of the Lord did not see, that is, did not suffer, as was predicted in prophecy: "Thou shall not suffer Thy Holy one to see corruption." For who denies that He was wounded by the piercing of the nails, and that He was stabbed with the lance? But even what is properly called by men corporeal corruption, that is, putrescence itself, if as yet there is anything left to consume, increases by the diminution of the good. But if corruption shall have absolutely consumed it, so that there is no good, no nature will remain, for there will be nothing that corruption may corrupt; and so there will not even be putrescence, for there will be nowhere at all for it to be.

Chapter 21. —From Measure Things are Said to Be Moderate-Sized.

Therefore, now by common usage things small and mean are said to have measure, because some measure remains in them, without which they would no longer be moderatesized, but would not exist at all. But those things that because of too much progress are called immoderate, are blamed for very excessiveness; but yet it is necessary that those things themselves be restrained in some manner under God who has disposed all things in extension, number, and weight.

Chapter 22. —Measure in Some Sense is Suitable to God Himself.

But God cannot be said to have measure, lest He should seem to be spoken of as limited. Yet He is not immoderate by whom measure is bestowed upon all things, so that they may in any measure exist. Nor again ought God to be called measured, as if He received measure from anyone. But if we say that He is the highest measure, by chance we say something; if indeed in speaking of the highest measure we mean the highest good. For every measure in so far as it is a measure is good; whence nothing can be called measured, modest, modified, without praise, although in another sense we use measure for limit, and speak of no measure where there is no limit, which is sometimes said with praise as when it is said: "And of His kingdom there shall be no limit." For it might also be said, "There shall be no measure," so that measure might be used in the sense of limit; for He who reigns in no measure, assuredly does not reign at all.

Chapter 23. —Whence a Bad Measure, a Bad Form, a Bad Order May Sometimes Be Spoken of.

Therefore a bad measure, a bad form, a bad order, are either so called because they are less than they should be, or because they are not adapted to those things to which they should be adapted; so that they may be called bad as being alien and incongruous; as if anyone should be said not to have done in a good measure because he has done less than he ought, or because he has done in such a thing as he ought not to have done, or more than was fitting, or not conveniently; so that the very fact of that being reprehended which is done in a bad measure, is justly reprehended for no other cause than that the measure is not there maintained. Likewise, a form is called bad either in comparison with something more handsome or more beautiful, this form being less, that greater, not in size but in comeliness; or because it is out of harmony with the thing to which it is applied, so that it seems alien and unsuitable. As if a man should walk forth into a public place naked, which nakedness does not offend if seen in a bath. Likewise, also order is called bad when order itself is maintained in an inferior degree. Hence not order, but rather disorder, is bad; since either the ordering is less than it should be, or not as it should be. Yet where there is any measure, any form, any order, there is some good and some nature; but where there is no measure, no form, no order, there is no good, no nature.

Chapter 24. —It is Proved by the Testimonies of Scripture that God is Unchangeable. The Son of God Begotten, Not Made.

Those things which our faith holds and which reason in whatever way has traced out, are fortified by the testimonies of the divine Scriptures, so that those who because of feebler intellect are not able to comprehend these things, may believe the divine authority, and so may deserve to know. But let not those who understand, but are less instructed in ecclesiastical literature, suppose that we set forth these things from our own intellect rather than what are in those Books. Accordingly, that God is unchangeable is written in the Psalms: "Thou shalt change them and they shall be changed; but Thou thyself art the same." And in the book of Wisdom, concerning wisdom: "Remaining in herself, she renews all things." Whence also the Apostle Paul: "To the invisible, incorruptible, only God." And the Apostle James: "Every best giving and every perfect gift is from above, descending from the Father of light, with whom there is no changeableness, neither obscuring of influence." Likewise, because what He begat of Himself is what He Himself is, it is said in brief by the Son Himself: "I and the Father are one." But because the Son was not made, since through Him were all things made, thus it is written: "In the beginning was the Word, and the Word was with God, and God was the Word; this was in the beginning with God. All things were made through Him, and without Him was made nothing;" that is, without Him was not anything made.

Chapter 25. —This Last Expression Misunderstood by Some.

For no attention should be paid to the ravings of men who think that nothing should be understood to mean something, and moreover think to compel anyone to vanity of this kind because nothing is placed at the end of the sentence. Therefore, they say, it was made, and because it was made, nothing is itself something. They have lost their senses by zeal in contradicting, and do not understand that it makes no difference whether it be said: "Without Him was made nothing," or "without Him nothing was made." For even if the order were the last mentioned, they could nevertheless say, that nothing is itself something because it was made. For in the case of what is in truth something, what difference does it make if it be said "Without him a house was made," so long as it is understood that something was made without him, which something is a house? So also because it is said: "Without Him was made nothing," since nothing is assuredly not anything, when it is truly and properly spoken, it makes no difference whether it be said: "Without Him was made nothing or Without Him nothing was made," or "nothing was made." But who cares to speak with men who can say of this very expression of mine "It makes no difference," "Therefore it makes some difference, for nothing itself is something?" But those whose brains are not addled, see it as a thing most manifest that this something is to be understood when it says, "It makes no difference," as when I say, "It matters in no respect." But these, if they should say to anyone, "What hast thou done?" and he should reply that he has done nothing, would, according to this mode of disputation, falsely accuse him saying, "Thou hast done something, therefore, because thou hast done nothing; for nothing is itself something." But they have also the Lord Himself placing this word at the end of a sentence, when He says: "And in secret have I spoken nothing." Let them read, therefore, and be silent.

Chapter 26. —That Creatures are Made of Nothing.

Because therefore God made all things which He did not beget of Himself, not of those things that already existed, but of those things that did not exist at all, that is, of nothing," the Apostle Paul says: "Who calls the things that are not as if they are." But still more plainly it is written in the book of Maccabees: "I pray thee, son, look at the heaven and the earth and all the things that are in them; see and know that it was not these of which the Lord God made us." And from this that is written in the Psalm: "He spoke, and they were made." It is manifest, that not of Himself He begat these things, but that He made them by word and command. But what is not of Himself is assuredly of nothing. For there was not anything of which he should make them, concerning which the apostle says most openly: "For from Him, and through Him, and in Him are all things."

Chapter 27. —"From Him" And "Of Him" Do Not Mean The Same Thing.

But "from Him" does not mean the same as "of Him." For what is of Him may be said to be from Him; but not everything that is from Him is rightly said to be of

Him. For from Him are heaven and earth, because He made them; but not of Him because they are not of His substance. As in the case of a man who begets a son and makes a house, from himself is the son, from himself is the house, but the son is of him, the house is of earth and wood. But this is so, because as a man he cannot make something even of nothing; but God of whom are all things, through whom are all things, in whom are all things, had no need of any material which He had not made to assist His omnipotence.

Chapter 28. —Sin Not From God, But From The Will of Those Sinning.

But when we hear: "All things are from Him, and through Him, and in Him," we ought assuredly to understand all natures which naturally exist. For sins, which do not preserve but vitiate nature, are not from Him; which sins, Holy Scripture in many ways testifies, are from the will of those sinning, especially in the passage where the apostle says: "But dost thou suppose this, O man, that judges those who do such things, and does them, that thou shall escape the judgment of God? Or dost thou despise the riches of His goodness, and patience, and long-suffering, not knowing that the patience of God leaded thee to repentance? But according to the hardness of thy heart and thy impenitent heart, thou treasures up for thyself wrath against the day of wrath and of the revelation of the just judgment of God, who will render unto everyone according to his works."

Chapter 29. —That God is Not Defiled by Our Sins.

And yet, though all things that He established are in Him, those who sin do not defile Him, of whose wisdom it is said: "She touches all things because of her purity, and nothing defiled assails her." For it behooves us to believe that as God is incorruptible and unchangeable, so also is He consequently undefilable.

Chapter 30. —That Good Things, Even the Least, and Those that are Earthly, are by God.

But that God made even the least things, that is, earthly and mortal things, must undoubtedly be understood from that passage of the apostle, where, speaking of the members of our flesh: "For if one member is glorified, all the members rejoice with it, and if one member suffers, all the members suffer with it;" also this he then says: "God has placed the members each one of them in the body as he willed;" and "God has tempered the body, giving to that to which it was wanting greater honor, that there should be no schism in the body, but that the members should have the same care one for another." But what the apostle thus praises in the measure and form and order of the members of the flesh, you find in the flesh of all animals, alike the greatest and the least; for all flesh is among earthly goods, and consequently is esteemed among the least.

Chapter 31. —To Punish and to Forgive Sins Belong Equally to God.

Likewise because it belongs to divine judgment, not human, what sort of punishment and how great is due to every fault, it is thus written: "O the height of the riches of the wisdom and the knowledge of God! how inscrutable are His judgments and his ways past finding out!" Likewise because by the goodness of God sins are forgiven to the converted, the very fact that Christ was sent sufficiently shows, who not in His own nature as God, but in our nature, which He assumed from a woman, died for us; which goodness of God with reference to us, and which love of God, the apostle thus sets forth: "But God commended His love toward us, in that while we were yet sinners Christ died for us; much more now being justified in His blood we shall be saved from wrath through Him. For if when we were enemies we were reconciled to God through the death of His Son, much more being reconciled we shall be saved in His life." But because even when due punishment is rendered to sinners, there is no unrighteousness on God's part, he thus says: "What shall we say? Is God unrighteous who visited with wrath?" But in one place he has briefly admonished that goodness and severity are alike from Him, saying: "Thou sees then the goodness and severity of God; toward them that have fallen, severity, but towards thee goodness, if thou should continue in goodness."

Chapter 32. —From God Also is the Very Power to Be Hurtful.

Likewise, because the power even of those that are hurtful is from God alone, thus it stands written, Wisdom speaking: "Through me kings reign and tyrants hold the land through me." The apostle also says: "For there is no power but of God." But that it is worthily done is written in the book of Job: "Who makes to reign a man that is a hypocrite, because the perversity of the people." And concerning the people of Israel God says: "I gave them a king in my wrath." For it is not unrighteous, that the wicked receiving the power of being hurtful, both the patience of the good should be proved and the iniquity of the evil punished. For through power given to the Devil both Job was proved so that he might appear righteous, and Peter was tempted lest he should be presumptuous, and Paul was buffeted lest he should be exalted, and Judas was damned so that he should hang himself. When, therefore, through the power which He has given the Devil, God Himself shall have done all things righteously, nevertheless punishment shall at last be rendered to the Devil not for these things justly done, but for the unrighteous willing to be hurtful, which belonged to himself, when it shall be said to the impious who persevered in consenting to his wickedness, "Go ye into everlasting fire which my God has prepared for the Devil and his angels."

Chapter 33. —That Evil Angels Have Been Made Evil, Not by God, But by Sinning.

But because evil angels also were not constituted

evil by God, but were made evil by sinning, Peter in his epistle says: "For if God spared not angels when they sinned, but casting them down into the dungeons of smoky hell, He delivered them to be reserved for punishment in judgment." Hence Peter shows that there is still due to them the penalty of the last judgment, concerning which the Lord says: "Go ye into everlasting fire, which has been prepared for the Devil and his angels." Although they have already penally received this hell, that is, an inferior smoky air as a prison, which nevertheless since it is also called heaven, is not that heaven in which there are stars, but this lower heaven by the smoke of which the clouds are conglobulated, and where the birds fly; for both a cloudy heaven is spoken of, and flying things are called heavenly. As when the Apostle Paul calls those evil angels, against whom as enemies by living piously we contend, "spiritual things of wickedness in heavenly places." That this may not be understood of the upper heavens, he plainly says elsewhere: "According to the presence of the prince of this air, who now worketh in the sons of disobedience."

Chapter 34. —That Sin is Not the Striving for an Evil Nature, But the Desertion of a Better.

Likewise because sin, or unrighteousness, is not the striving after evil nature but the desertion of better, it is thus found written in the Scriptures: "Every creature of God is good." And accordingly, every tree also which God planted in Paradise is assuredly good. Man did not therefore strive after an evil nature when he touched the forbidden tree; but by deserting what was better, he committed an evil deed. Since the Creator is better than any creature which He has made, His command should not have been deserted, that the thing forbidden, however good, might be touched; since the better having been deserted, the good of the creature was striven for, which was touched contrary to the command of the Creator. God did not plant an evil tree in Paradise; but He Himself was better who prohibited its being touched.

Chapter 35. —The Tree Was Forbidden to Adam Not Because It Was Evil, But Because It Was Good for Man to Be Subject to God.

For besides, He had made the prohibition, in order to show that the nature of the rational soul ought not to be in its own power, but in subjection to God, and that it guards the order of its salvation through obedience, corrupting it through disobedience. Hence also He called the tree, the touching of which He forbade, the tree "of the knowledge of good and evil;" because when man should have touched it in the face of the prohibition, he would experience the penalty of sin, and so would know the difference between the good of obedience, and the evil of disobedience.

Chapter 36. —No Creature of God is Evil, But to Abuse a Creature of God is Evil.

For who is so foolish as to think a creature of God, especially one planted in Paradise, blameworthy; when indeed not even thorns and thistles, which the earth brought forth, according to the judiciary judgment of God, for wearing out the sinner in labor, should be blamed? For even such herbs have their measure and form and order, which whoever considers soberly will find praiseworthy; but they are evil to that nature which ought thus to be restrained as a recompense for sin. Therefore, as I have said, sin is not the striving after an evil nature, but the desertion of a better, and so the deed itself is evil, not the nature which the sinner uses amiss. For it is evil to use amiss that which is good. Whence the apostle reproves certain ones as condemned by divine judgment, "Who have worshipped and served the creature more than the Creator." He does not reprove the creature, which he who should do would act injuriously towards the Creator, but those who, deserting the better, have used amiss the good.

Chapter 37. —God Makes Good Use of the Evil Deeds of Sinners.

Accordingly, if all natures should guard their own proper measure and form and order, there would be no evil: but if anyone should wish to misuse these good things, not even thus does he vanquish the will of God, who knows how to order righteously even the unrighteous; so that if they themselves through the iniquity of their will should misuse His good things, He through the righteousness of His power may use their evil deeds, rightly ordaining to punishment those who have perversely ordained themselves to sins.

Chapter 38. —Eternal Fire Torturing the Wicked, Not Evil.

For neither is eternal fire itself, which is to torture the impious, an evil nature, since it has its measure, its form and its order depraved by no iniquity; but it is an evil torture for the damned, to whose sins it is due. For neither is yonder light, because it tortures the bleareyed, an evil nature.

Chapter 39. —Fire is Called Eternal, Not as God Is, But Because Without End.

But fire is eternal, not as God is eternal, because, though without end, yet is not without beginning; but God is also without beginning. Then, although it may be employed perpetually for the punishment of sinners, yet it is mutable nature. But that is true eternity which is true immortality, that is that highest immutability, which cannot be changed at all. For it is one thing not to suffer change, when change is possible, and another thing to be absolutely incapable of change. Therefore, just as man is called good, yet not as God, of whom it was said, "There is none good save God alone;" and just as the soul is called immortal, yet not as God, of whom it was said, "Who alone hath immortality;" and just as a man is called wise, yet not as God, of whom it was said, "To God the only wise;" so fire is called eternal, yet not as God, whose alone is immortality itself and true eternity.

Chapter 40. —Neither Can God Suffer Hurt, Nor Any Other, Save by the Just Ordination of God.

Since these things are so, according to the Catholic faith, and wholesome doctrine, and truth perspicuous to those of good understanding, neither can anyone hurt the nature of God, nor can the nature of God unrighteously hurt anyone, or suffer any one to do hurt with impunity. "For he that doeth hurt shall receive," says the apostle, "according to the hurt that he has done; and there is no accepting of persons with God."

Chapter 41. —How Great Good Things the Manichæans Put in the Nature of Evil, and How Great Evil Things in the Nature of Good.

But if the Manichæans were willing, without pernicious zeal for defending their error, and with the fear of God, to think, they would not most criminally blaspheme by supposing two natures, the one good, which they call God, the other evil, which God did not make: so erring, so delirious, nay so insane, are they that they do not see, that even in what they call the nature of supreme evil they place so great good things: life, power, safety, memory, intellect, temperance, virtue, plenty, sense, light, suavity, extensions, numbers, peace, measure, form, order; but in what they call supreme good, so many evil things: death, sickness, forgetfulness, foolishness, confusion, impotence, need, stolidity, blindness, pain, unrighteousness, disgrace, war, intemperance, deformity, perversity. For they say that the princes of darkness also have been alive in their own nature, and in their own kingdom were safe, and remembered and understood. For they say that the Prince of Darkness harangued in such a manner, that neither could he have said such things, nor could he have been heard by those by whom he was said to have been heard, without memory and understanding; and to have had a temper suitable to his mind and body, and to have ruled by virtue of power, and to have had abundance and fruitfulness with respect to his elements, and they are said to have perceived themselves mutually and the light as near at hand, and to have had eyes by which they could see the light afar off; which eyes assuredly could not have seen the light without some light (whence also they are rightly called light); and they are said to have enjoyed exceedingly the sweetness of their pleasures, and to have been determined by measured members and dwelling-places. But unless there had been some sort of beauty there, they would not have loved their wives, nor would their bodies have been steady by adaptation of parts; without which, those things could not have been done there which the Manichæans insanely say were done. And unless some peace had been there, they would not have obeyed their Prince. Unless measure had been there, they would have done nothing else than eat or drink, or rage, or whatever they might have done, without any society: although not even those that did these things would have had determinate forms, unless measure had been there. But now the Manichæans say that they did such things that they cannot be denied having had in all their actions measures suitable to themselves. But if form had not been there, no natural quality would have there subsisted. But if there had been no order there, some would not have ruled, others been ruled; they would not have lived harmoniously in their element; in fine, they would not have had their members adapted to their places, so that they could not do all those things that the Manichæans vainly fable. But if they say that God's nature does not die, what according to their vanity does Christ raise from the dead? If they say that it does not grow sick, what does He cure? If they say that it is not subject to forgetfulness, what does He remind? If they say that it is not deficient in wisdom, what does He teach? If they say that it is not confused, what does He restore? If they say that it was not vanquished and taken captive, what does He liberate? If they say that it was not in need, to what does He minister aid? If they say that it did not lose feeling, what does He animate? If they say that it has not been blinded, what does He illuminate? If it is not in pain, to what does He give relief? If it is not unrighteous, what does He correct through precepts? If it is not in disgrace, what does He cleanse? If it is not in war, to what does He promise peace? If it is not deficient in moderation, upon what does He impose the measure of law? If it is not deformed, what does He reform? If it is not perverse, what does He emend? For all these things done by Christ, they say, are to be attributed not to that thing which was made by God, and which has become depraved by its own free choice in sinning, but to the very nature, yea to the very substance of God, which is what God Himself is.

Chapter 42. —Manichæan Blasphemies Concerning the Nature of God.

What can be compared to those blasphemies? Absolutely nothing, unless the errors of other sectaries be considered; but if that error be compared with itself in another aspect, of which we have not yet spoken, it will be convicted of far worse and more execrable blasphemy. For they say that some souls, which they will have to be of the substance of God and of absolutely the same nature, which have not sinned of their own accord, but have been overcome and oppressed by the race of darkness, which they call evil, for combating which they descended not of their own accord, but at the command of the Father, are fettered forever in the horrible sphere of darkness. So according to their sacrilegious vaporings, God liberated Himself in a certain part from a great evil, but again condemned Himself in another part, which He could not liberate, and triumphed over the enemy itself as if it had been vanquished from above. O criminal, incredible audacity, to believe, to speak, to proclaim such things about God! Which when they endeavor to defend, that with their eyes shut they may rush headlong into yet worse things, they say that the commingling of the evil nature does these things, in order that the good nature of God may suffer so great evils: for that this good nature in its own sphere could or can suffer no one of these things.

As if a nature were lauded as incorruptible, because it does not hurt itself, and not because it cannot suffer hurt from another. Then if the nature of God hurt the nature of darkness, and the nature of darkness hurt the nature of God, there are therefore two evil things which hurt each other in turn, and the race of darkness was the better disposed, because if it committed hurt it did it unwillingly; for it did not wish to commit hurt, but to enjoy the good which belonged to God. But God wished to extinguish it, as Manichæus most openly raves forth in his epistle of the ruinous Foundation. For forgetting that he had shortly before said: "But His most resplendent realms were so founded upon the shining and happy land, that they could never be either moved or shaken by anyone;" he afterwards said: "But the Father of the most blessed light, knowing that great ruin and desolation which would arise from the darkness, threaten his holy worlds, unless he should send in opposition a deity excellent and renowned, mighty in strength, by whom he might at the same time overcome and destroy the race of darkness, which having been extinguished, the inhabitants

Concerning the Nature of Good, Against the Manichaeans

of light would enjoy perpetual rest." Behold, he feared ruin and desolation that threatened his worlds! Assuredly they were so founded upon the shining and happy land that they never could be either moved or shaken by anyone? Behold, from fear he wished to hurt the neighboring race, which he endeavored to destroy and extinguish, in order that the inhabitants of light might enjoy perpetual rest. Why did he not add, and perpetual bondage? Were not these souls that he fettered forever in the sphere of darkness, the inhabitants of light, of whom he says plainly, that "they have suffered themselves to err from their former bright nature?" when against his will he is compelled to say, that they sinned by free will, while he wishes to ascribe sin only to the necessity of the contrary nature: everywhere ignorant what to say, and as if he were himself already in the sphere of darkness which he invented, seeking, and not finding, how he may escape. But let him say what he will to the seduced and miserable men by whom he is honored far more highly than Christ, that at this price he may sell to them such long and sacrilegious fables. Let him say what he will, let him shut up, as it were, in a sphere, as in a prison, the race of darkness, and let him fasten outside the nature of light, to which he promised perpetual rest on the extinction of the enemy: behold, the penalty of light is worse than that of darkness; the penalty of the divine nature is worse than that of the adverse race. But since although the latter is in the midst of darkness it pertains to its nature to dwell in darkness; but souls which are the very same thing that God is, cannot be received, he says, into those peaceful realms, and are alienated from the life and liberty of the holy light, and are fettered in the aforesaid horrible sphere: whence he says, "Those souls shall adhere to the things that they have loved, having been left in the same sphere of darkness, bringing this upon themselves by their own deserts." Is not this assuredly free voluntary choice? See how insanely he ignores what he says, and by making self-contradictory statements wages a worse war against himself than against the God of the race of darkness itself. Accordingly, if the souls of light are damned, because they loved darkness, the race of darkness, which loved light, is unjustly damned. And the race of darkness indeed loved light from the beginning, violently, it may be, but yet so as to wish for its possession, not its extinction: but the nature of light wished to extinguish in war the darkness; therefore when vanquished it loved darkness. Choose which you will: whether it was compelled by necessity to love darkness, or seduced by free will. If by necessity, wherefore is it damned? if by free will, wherefore is the nature of God involved in so great iniquity? If the nature of God was compelled by necessity to love darkness, it did not vanquish, but was vanquished: if by free will, why do the wretches hesitate any longer to attribute the will to sin to the nature which God made out of nothing, lest they should thereby attribute it to the light which He begat?

Chapter 43. —Many Evils Before His Commingling with Evil are Attributed to the Nature of God by the Manichæans.

What if we should also show that before the commingling of evil, which stupid fable they have most madly believed, great evils were in what they call the nature of light? what will it seem possible to add to these blasphemies? For before the conflict, there was the hard and inevitable necessity of fighting: here is truly a great evil, before evil is commingled with good. Let them say whence this is, when as yet no commingling had taken place? But if there was no necessity, there was therefore free will: whence also this so great evil, that God himself should wish to hurt his own nature, which could not be hurt by the enemy, by sending it to be cruelly commingled, to be basely purged, to be unjustly damned? Behold, the great evil of a pernicious, noxious, and savage will, before any evil from the contrary nature was mingled with it! Or perchance he did not know that this would happen to his members, that they should love darkness and become hostile to holy light, as Manichæus says, that is, not only to their own God, but also to the Father from whom they had their being? Whence therefore this so great evil of ignorance, before any evil from the nature of darkness was mingled with it? But if he knew that this would happen, either there was in him everlasting cruelty, if he did not grieve over the contamination and damnation of his own nature that was to take place, or everlasting misery, if he did so grieve: whence also this so great evil of your supreme good before any commingling with your supreme evil? Assuredly that part of the nature itself which was fettered in the eternal chain of that sphere, if it knew not that this fate awaited it, even so was there everlasting ignorance in the nature of God, but if it knew, then everlasting misery: whence this so great evil before any evil from the contrary nature was commingled? Or perchance did it, in the greatness of its love (charity), rejoice that through its punishment perpetual rest was prepared for the residue of the inhabitants of light? Let him who sees how abominable it is to say this, pronounce an anathema. But if this should be done so that at least the good nature itself should not become hostile to the light, it might be possible, perchance, not for the nature of God indeed, but for some man, as it were, to be regarded as praiseworthy, who for the sake of his country should be willing to suffer something of evil, which evil indeed could be only for a time, and not forever: but now also they speak of that fettering in the sphere of darkness as eternal, and not indeed of a certain thing but of the nature of God; and assuredly it were a most unrighteous, and execrable, and ineffably sacrilegious joy, if the nature of God rejoiced that it should love darkness, and should become hostile to holy light. Whence this so monstrous and abominable evil before any evil from the contrary nature was commingled? Who can endure insanity so perverse and so impious, as to attribute so great good things to supreme evil, and so great evils to supreme good, which is God?

Chapter 44. —Incredible Turpitudes in God Imagined by Manichæus.

But now when they speak of that part of the nature of God as everywhere mixed up in heaven, in earth, in all bodies dry and moist, in all sorts of flesh, in all seeds of trees, herbs, men, and animals: not as present by the power of divinity, for administering and ruling all things, undefilably, inviolably, incorruptibly, without any connection with them, which we say of God; but fettered, oppressed, polluted, to be loosed and liberated, as they say, not only through the running to and fro of the sun and the moon, and through the powers of light, but also through their Elect: what sacrilegious and incredible turpitudes this kind of error recommends to them even if it does not induce them to accept, it is horrible to speak of. For they say that the powers of light are transformed into beautiful males and are set over against the women of the race of darkness; and that the same powers again are transformed into beautiful females and are set over against the males of the race of darkness; that through their beauty they enkindle the foulest lust of the princes of darkness, and in this manner vital substance, that is, the nature of God, which they say is held fettered in their bodies, having been loosed from their members relaxed through lust, flies away, and when it has been taken up or cleansed, is liberated. This the wretches read, this they say, this they hear, this they believe, this they put as follows, in the seventh book of their Thesaurus(for so they call a certain writing of Manichæus, in which these blasphemies stand written): "Then the blessed Father, who has bright ships, little apartments, dwelling-places, or magnitudes, according to his indwelling clemency, brings the help by which he is drawn out and liberated from the impious bonds, straits, and torments of his vital substance. And so by his own invisible nod he transforms those powers of his, which are held in this most brilliant ship, and makes them to bring forth adverse powers, which have been arranged in the various tracts of the heavens. Since these consist of both sexes, male and female, he orders the aforesaid powers to bring forth partly in the form of beardless youths, for the adverse race of females, partly in the form of bright maidens, for the contrary race of males: knowing that all these hostile powers because the deadly and most foul lust innate in them, are very easily taken captive, delivered up to these most beautiful forms which appear, and in this manner they are dissolved. But you may know that this same blessed Father of ours is identical with his powers, which for a necessary reason he transforms into the undefiled likeness of youths and maidens. But these he uses as his own arms, and through them he accomplishes his will. But there are bright ships full of these divine powers, which are stationed after the likeness of marriage over against the infernal races, and who with alacrity and ease effect at the very moment what they have planned. Therefore, when reason demands that these same holy powers should appear to males, straightway also they show by their dress the likeness of most beautiful maidens. Again when females are to be dealt with, putting aside the forms of maidens, they show the forms of beardless youths. But by this handsome appearance of theirs, ardor and lust increase, and in this way the chain of their worst thoughts is loosed, and the living soul which was held by their members, relaxed by this occasion escapes, and is mingled with its own most pure air; when the souls thoroughly cleansed ascend to the bright ships, which have been prepared for conveying them and for ferrying them over to their own country. But that which still bears the stains of the adverse race, descends little by little through billows and fires, and is mingled with trees and other plants and with all seeds, and is plunged into divers fires. And in what manner the figures of youths and maidens from that great and most glorious ship appear to the contrary powers which live in the heavens and have a fiery nature; and from that handsome appearance, part of the life which is held in their members having been released is conducted away through fires into the earth: in the same manner also, that most high power, which dwells in the ship of vital waters appears in the likeness of youths and holy maidens to those powers whose nature is cold and moist, and which are arranged in the heavens. And indeed to those that are females, among these the form of youths appears, but to the males, the form of maidens. By his changing and diversity of divine and most beautiful persons, the princes male and female of the moist and cold race are loosed, and what is vital in them escapes; but whatever should remain, having been relaxed, is conducted into the earth through cold, and is mingled with all the races of darkness" Who can endure this? Who can believe, not indeed that it is true, but that it could even be said? Behold those who fear to anathematize Manichæus teaching these things, and do not fear to believe in a God doing them and suffering them!

Chapter 45. —Certain Unspeakable Turpitudes Believed, Not Without Reason, Concerning the Manichæans Themselves.

But they say, that through their own Elect that same commingled part and nature of God is purged, by eating and drinking forsooth, (because they say that it is held fettered in all foods); that when they are taken up by the Elect for the nourishment of the body in eating and drinking, it is loosed, sealed, and liberated through their sanctity. Nor do the wretches pay heed to the fact that this is believed about them not without good reason, and they deny it in vain, so long as they do not anathematize the books of Manichæus and cease to be Manichæans. For if, as they say, a part of God is fettered in all seeds, and is purged by eating on the part of the Elect; who may not properly believe, that they do what they read in the Thesaurus was done among the powers of heaven and the princes of darkness; since indeed they say that their flesh is also from the race of darkness, and since they do not hesitate to believe and to affirm that the vital substance fettered in them is a part of God? Which assuredly if it is to be loosed, and purged by eating, as their lamentable error compels them to acknowledge; who does not see, who does not shudder at the greatness and the unspeakableness of what follows?

Chapter 46. —The Unspeakable Doctrine of the Fundamental Epistle.

For they even say that Adam, the first man, was created by certain princes of darkness so that the light might be held by them lest it should escape. For in the epistle which they call Fundamental, Manichæus wrote as follows respecting the way in which the Prince of Darkness, whom they represent as the father of the first man, spoke to the rest of his allied princes of darkness, and how he acted: "Therefore with wicked inventions he said to those present: What does this huge light that is rising seem to you to be? See how the pole moves, how it shakes most of the powers. Wherefore it is right for me rather to ask you beforehand for whatever light you have in your powers: since thus I will form an image of that great one who has appeared in his glory, through which we may be able to rule, freed in some measure from the conversation of darkness. Hearing these things, and deliberating for a long time among themselves, they thought it most just to furnish what was demanded of them. For they did not have confidence in being able to retain the light that they had forever; hence they thought it better to offer it to their Prince, by no means without hope that in this way they would rule. It must be considered therefore how they furnished the light that they had. For this also is scattered throughout all the divine scriptures and the heavenly secrets; but to the wise it is easy enough to know how it was given: for it is known immediately and openly by him who should truly and faithfully wish to consider. Since there was a promiscuous throng of those who had come together, females and males of course, he impelled them to copulate among themselves: in which copulation the males emitted seed, the females were made pregnant. But the offspring were like those who had begotten them, the first obtaining as it were the largest portion of the parents' strength. Taking these as a special gift their Prince rejoiced. And just as even now we see take place, that the nature of evil taking thence strength forms the fashioner of bodies, so also the aforesaid Prince, taking the offspring of his companions, which had the senses of their parents, sagacity, light, procreated at the same time with themselves in the process of generation, devoured them; and very many powers having been taken from food of this kind, in which there was present not only fortitude, but much more astuteness and depraved sensibilities from the ferocious race of the progenitors, he called his own spouse to himself, springing from the same stock as himself, emitted, like the rest the abundance of evils that he had devoured, himself also adding something from his own thought and power, so that his disposition became the former and arranger of all the things that he had poured forth; whose consort received these things as soil cultivated in the best way is accustomed to receive seed. For in her were constructed and woven together the images of all heavenly and earthly powers, so that what was formed obtained the likeness, so to speak, of a full orb."

Chapter 47. —He Compels to the Perpetration of Horrible Turpitudes.

O abominable monster! O execrable perdition and ruin of deluded souls! I am not speaking of the blasphemy of saying these things about the nature of God which is thus fettered. Let the wretches deluded and hunted by deadly error give heed to this at least, that if a part of their God is fettered by the copulation of males and females which they profess to loose and purge by eating it, the necessity of this unspeakable error compels them not only to loose and purge the part of God from bread and vegetables and fruits, which alone they are seen publicly to partake of, but also from that which might be fettered through copulation, if conception should take place. That they do this some are said to have confessed before a public tribunal, not only in Paphlagonia, but also in Gaul, as I heard in Rome from a certain Catholic Christian; and when they were asked by the authority of what writing they did these things, they betrayed this fact concerning the Thesaurus that I have just mentioned. But when this is cast in their teeth, they are in the habit of replying, that some enemy or other has withdrawn from their number, that is from the number of their Elect, and has made a schism, and has founded a most foul heresy of this kind. Whence it is manifest that even if they do not themselves practice this thing, some who do practice it do it on the basis of their books. Therefore let them reject the books, if they abhor the crime, which they are compelled to commit, if they hold to the books; or if they do not commit them, they endeavor in opposition to the books to live more purely. But what do they do when it is said to them, either purge the light from whatever seeds you can, so that you cannot refuse to do that which you assert that you do not do; or else anathematize Manichæus, when he says that a part of God is in all seeds, and that it is fettered by copulation, but that whatever of light, that is, of the aforesaid part of God, should become the food of the Elect, is purged by being eaten. Do you see what he compels you to believe, and do you still hesitate to anathematize him? What do they do, I say, when this is said to them? To what subterfuges do they betake themselves, when either so nefarious a doctrine is to be anathematized, or so nefarious a turpitude committed, in comparison with which all those intolerable evils to which I have already called attention, seem tolerable, namely, that they say of the nature of God that it was pressed by necessity to wage war, that it was either secure by everlasting ignorance, or was disturbed by everlasting grief and fear, when the corruption of commingling and the chain of everlasting damnation should come upon it, that finally as a result of the conflict it should be taken captive, oppressed, polluted, that after a false victory it should be fettered forever in a horrible sphere and separated from its original blessedness, while if considered in themselves they cannot be endured?

Chapter 48. —Augustin Prays that the Manichæans May Be Restored to Their Senses.

O great is Thy patience, Lord, full of compassion and gracious, slow to anger, and plenteous in mercy, and true; who makes Thy sun to rise upon the good and the evil, and who sends rain upon the just and the unjust; who wills not the death of the sinner, so much as that he return and live; who reproving in parts, dost give place to repentance, that wickedness having been abandoned, they may believe on Thee, O Lord; who by Thy patience dost lead to repentance, although many according to the hardness of their heart and their impenitent heart treasure up for themselves wrath against the day of wrath and of the revelation of Thy righteous judgment, who will render to every man according to his works; who in the day when a man shall have turned from his iniquity to Thy mercy and truth, wilt forget all his iniquities: stand before us, grant unto us that through our ministry, by which Thou hast been pleased to refute this execrable and too horrible error, as many have already been liberated, many also may be liberated, and whether through the sacrament of Thy holy baptism, or through the sacrifice of a broken spirit and a contrite and humbled heart, in the sorrow of repentance, they may deserve to receive the remission of their sins and blasphemies, by which through ignorance they have offended Thee. For nothing is of any avail, save Thy surpassing mercy and power, and the truth of Thy baptism, and the keys of the kingdom of heaven in Thy holy Church; so that we must not despair of men as long as by Thy patience they live on this earth, who even knowing how great an evil it is to think or to say such things about Thee, are detained in that malign profession on account of the use or the attainment of temporal or earthly convenience, if rebuked by Thy reproaches they in any way flee to Thy ineffable goodness, and prefer to all the enticements of the carnal life, the heavenly and eternal life.

www.ingramcontent.com/pod-product-compliance
Lightning Source LLC
Chambersburg PA
CBHW052044070526
44584CB00018B/2597